GABY ARRIAGA

NEAR FUTURE THINKING®

**THE DIFFERENCE BETWEEN LEADING TRENDS
OR BEING DRAGGED ALONG BY THEM**

Near Future Thinking®
The Difference Between Leading Trends
Or Being Dragged Along By Them.

Second edition in English.
ISBN: 978-1-957973-54-8
Copyright © 2022 by Gabriela Arriaga Gutiérrez.

Editing: Elena Bazán.
Editorial Coordination: Denisse Zuñiga López.
Style Correction: Álvaro Martín and Alma Martínez.
Adaptation from Spanish to English: Salvador Lara.
Translation: Caitlin Cooper.
Illustration and Cover Design: Alee Baes.
Editorial Design: Tian Yuan and Alma Muñoz Cid.
Photo of the Author: Karla P. Acosta R.

Published and printed in Mexico.
www.Leonardo1452.com

AUTHOR BIO

Gaby Arriaga is the founder of Leonardo1452, a consulting company that specializes in consumer trends, and creator of the Near Future Thinking® framework. She has completed studies at Tecnológico de Monterrey, CEDIM and ITAM in Mexico City, EADA in Barcelona, Spain and the University of Austin in Texas, USA.

In 2009 Gaby founded Leonardo1452, the only company of its kind in Mexico, consulting for companies such as Google, YouTube, Diageo, Mondeléz, Kellogg's, Nestlé, Discovery Channel, and PepsiCo, among others. With her TrendAcademy® program, she trains companies in Latin America and Spain on how to apply Near Future Thinking® in their businesses. An international conference speaker, Gaby has presented in multiple countries throughout Latin America, the United Kingdom and Spain, alongside some of the most important business leaders in the world, such as Martin Lindstrom. Gaby has been a judge for awards such as EFFIE and the World Independent Advertising Awards in Los Angeles, California. In addition, she served as co-president of Account Planning Group (APG) Mexico, guest columnist for the business news website Expansión - CNN and weekly commentator on the television program Nuestro Día (Cadena Tres) where she talked about the most important trends in Mexico.

LinkedIn: Gaby Arriaga
Twitter: @gabysun

FOREWORD

To everyone who has accompanied me along the uncharted and winding (for me) path to publishing this book. To my parents, Ofelia and José Luis, who understood, among other things, that on several occasions I had to sacrifice family time to stay home and write. To my sister Sandra, who worked with me for years to pave the way for Leonardo1452, and who was my pillar when I faltered, because together we laid the foundations of this book. To my life partner Erika, who stood by me when I came home frustrated because someone told me "no," who helped me to find a "yes," and who stayed up many nights to read through the drafts I had asked her to read. To my team, who for years has listened to me talk about "the book," paddling along with me until I finally had it in my hands and made it "our book." To everyone who approached me with advice, a helpful contact or an "I want to read it already." To life itself, for giving me the opportunity to write down what I have discovered over the years. To you, reader, for choosing this book as part of your professional training, because yes, it was made just for you.

ACKNOWLEDGEMENTS

Although I am its author, this book was made possible from the work of the Trendhunters at Leonardo1452. Many thanks to you, accomplices of this dream, for the countless hours spent reading news, researching, deciphering data, attending conferences, analyzing videos, listening to consumer opinions, debating theories, drawing diagrams, and responding to the ever-changing challenges that our clients put in front of us. I am forever grateful for your boundless energy to transform what we discover together into a workshop, a podcast, a webinar, a social media story, a conference, a booklet, an infographic, a presentation, a video, a booth, a city tour, a board game, a play, and now...a book!!!! It was about time that this, our book, with our work, went out into the world. Let's jump aboard, Trendhunters, and let it lead us on new adventures.

CONTENT

INTRODUCTION

Why this book?

Companies ask for our help to be the most innovative, coolest, and trendiest; the brand that changes the rules of the game in their industry and gets named "revolutionary" by the media.

At Leonardo1452, we have written dozens of trend reports. Yet, our experience has shown that a document is not enough to anticipate the market.

We need to know how current events are unfolding in order to predict the future of a trend. For this reason, we have become specialists in the immediate horizon, the near future scenarios that give rise to a new way of thinking: Near Future Thinking®.

Leonardo1452 has detected trends in their very early stages including:

Vida de barrio®. In 2012, we foresaw that in certain areas of Mexico City, families would soon be able to meet their daily needs without having to venture outside their own neighborhoods. We saw how several young families started to resolve their day-to-day within the immediate perimeter of their homes, giving priority to a better quality of life and avoiding long, inefficient travel times. Most of the establishments of the new "Vida de barrio®" (Neighborhood Living) trend can be reached on foot, by bicycle or within a few subway stations.

Arriba los Pepes y los Toños®. (Long Live the Moms and Pops) A trend that favors buying locally and within our neighborhood. Priorities shifted to prefer stores owned by local residents rather than franchises owned by foreign companies.

Hogares Fabergé®. Just like the famous eggs created by the Russian jewelry artisans Fabergé, most of which feature tiny exquisite details in a very small space, modern dwellings have begun to take on a Fabergé form: where homes are increasingly smaller in size, inhabitants make use of every cubic centimeter by creating multifunctional spaces. For instance, dining rooms that also serve as offices for those who work from home (better known as home office), and modular furniture. We are beginning to see Fabergé® Homes in megacities such as Mexico City and we will continue to monitor this trend as it expands to other urban areas in Mexico and around the world.

Near Future Thinking®: Being alert to when a minority habit becomes a majority habit.

Eager to put our method to work, we created TrendAcademy® to teach others how trends take hold and to incorporate the theories of great sociologists, journalists, futurists and trend experts, such as Malcolm Gladwell, Everett M. Rogers, William Higham, Rohit Bhargava and Marian Salzman. By turning theoretical knowledge into practical exercises, we have developed a toolkit for business decision makers that encourages participants to stop focusing only on present-day challenges and to start thinking about the near future.

There is no better way to understand a trend than to identify it firsthand.

· Here we will see how a consumer trend behaves like a wave in the ocean. At first invisible, it gains height and volume as it approaches the beach until it breaks with force and disperses, leaving all the surrounding sand wet. This book explains how a trend takes shape and, according to your company profile, where you should be positioned when the wave breaks.

Think of this book as that talk a surf instructor would give you at the shoreline - about the physics behind the waves, where to start according to your age and level of experience, and what to do if you want to go pro.

In the same way, I will explain how a trend forms and, according to your company profile, where you should position yourself: when the trend is just starting to form, at its point of greatest visibility, or when it has already passed its peak. All of these positions are valid. It just depends on the brand and the company behind it.

1. NEAR FUTURE THINKING®: TO ANALYZE A TREND IS TO ANALYZE THE NEAR FUTURE

Studying trends is about much more than listing new cars, cell phones or furniture under the headline "trends."

Dr. Joseph Voros, a futures researcher, thinker and teacher based in Australia, divides futures into a cone-shaped graph now known as the Voroscope[1], from which I highlight the following four elements:

Preferable: what we would like to happen.

Possible: anything we can imagine that defies what we know today, such as the laws of physics.

Plausible: scenarios that could happen. These are based on what we know at present, such as gravity or the capabilities of human beings.

Probable: situations that are likely to happen because they are already happening in some way. This is the logical continuation of a situation that is already occurring.

Dr. Voros gives the example of J. F. Kennedy's ambition of reaching the Moon as an example of a preferable future. When he posed this future in 1961, it was only possible, since it was imaginable but it was not yet known how. Then, the technical knowledge was acquired to make that future plausible and eventually probable[2]. In this example, the probable scenarios are situations that arise as we get closer to the present.

It's like traveling in a vehicle that travels forward in time. The scenarios closest to our vehicle are the most probable, because we can see signs in the present - behaviors, conditions, knowledge, patterns - that give us certainty about reaching that near future, or it reaching us, in the way we envision it.

One possible and preferable scenario is for Mexico to win twenty gold medals at the 2036 Olympics. This is a future that we would like to see happen but one that seems to defy everything we currently know about sports in Mexico, but that, if the conditions are created, could be a plausible and eventually probable scenario.

A probable scenario in Mexico City is that all new homes, regardless of socioeconomic status, will measure less than 100 meters squared. This is a plausible scenario, due to overpopulation and the fact that more and more apartments are built every day. Currently, up to ten families now live in the same surface area that was once occupied by a single family.

1. Voros, Joseph, "The Futures Cone, use and history," 2017, <https://thevoroscope.com/2017/02/24/the-futures-cone-use-and-history/>.
2. Voros, Joseph, Swinburne University of Technology, "A Primer on Futures Studies, Foresight and the Use of Scenarios," 2001.

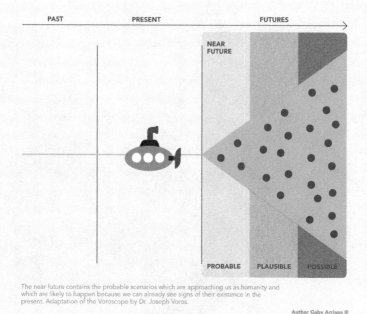

The near future contains the probable scenarios which are approaching us as humanity and which are likely to happen because we can already see signs of their existence in the present. Adaptation of the Voroscope by Dr. Joseph Voros.

Author Gaby Arriaga ©

Near Future Thinking® is recognizing these near future scenarios and preparing for them.

Many companies have a hard time envisioning the near future because they always want to cater to the big slice of the data pie, as they know that's where the sales are. They only look at the small slice when it's no longer there - when it's too late.

It is imperative for all companies to look into the near future, learn how to identify a trend on their own and establish their own trend spotting area, i.e. Trendhunting or Near Future Thinking®.

2. HOW TRENDS HAVE BEEN EXPLAINED UP UNTIL NOW

NEW TREND ADOPTERS
AGGREGATED VS ABSOLUTE

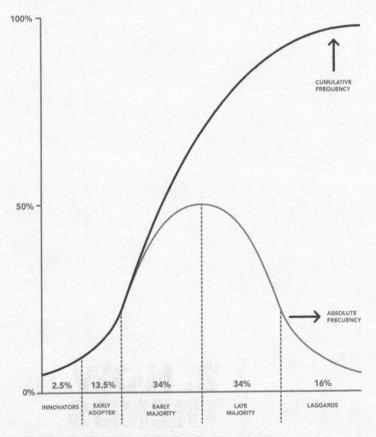

Adapted from Everett M. Rogers, *Diffusion of Innovations*.

Author Gaby Arriaga ©

The primary model used to date has been the "Diffusion of Innovations" theory by sociologist and professor Everett M. Rogers[1].

Rogers identified five profiles of people in terms of how quickly they accept and adopt new behaviors: first are the innovators, followed by the early adopters; then come the early majority and the late majority who embrace that behavior, and finally the laggards, who are more reluctant to change.

In addition, we can draw another curve in the form of an S which indicates that when these four profile groups have adopted a behavior, then the totality of a market or population has been met.

THE PROBLEM WITH THE TREND ADOPTION CURVE

At Leonardo 1452, Everett M. Rogers's model has been the starting point from which we explain how a consumer trend evolves in a given industry; however, we have come to realize that there are important caveats and tweaks to Rogers's theory.

- The size of each consumer belongs to one group, then they cannot be part of any other group. You can draw as many curves as you spot trends, and in each curve a consumer may belong to only one group or another.
- One might think that if a consumer belongs to one group, then they cannot be part of any other group. You can draw as many curves as you spot trends, and in each curve a consumer may belong to only one group or another.
- It seems that the story of a trend's development can be cut with a knife. It is very difficult to pinpoint at what millimeter and second the trend began to emerge.
- The S-shaped curve shows that when you reach the group of laggards, you have covered 100% of the market. This would lead you to think that if you reach that point as a company, you are the absolute market leader. This is not the case, because as the trend advances from one group to the next, more companies enter the competition.

A TREND IS LIKE A WAVE IN THE OCEAN.

1. Waves are primarily generated by the wind. The water gets pushed downward and upward creating these liquid swells. The wind represents the val-

---

1. Rogers, Everett M., Diffusion of Innovations, 5.ª ed., 2003.

ues and beliefs in society.

2. Underneath these swells, the water begins to move in a circular motion. This could be likened to the early market.

3. When the ripples near the shore, they create the waves that we see rising above sea level. It becomes evident that something was building under the water. Massive early market.

4. After this steep rise in the water comes the explosive release of energy that had been traveling long distances. Late mass market.

5. Once the wave has broken, the water continues to move forward, but with less and less force and diminishing energy. Laggard market

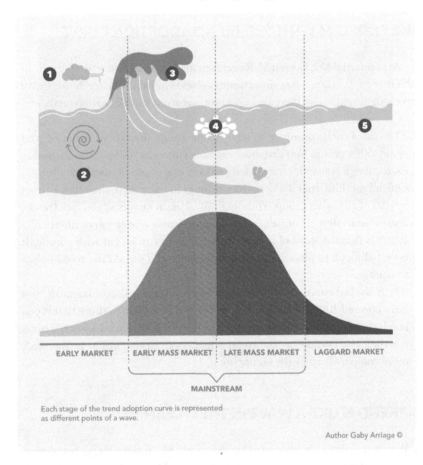

Each stage of the trend adoption curve is represented as different points of a wave.

Author Gaby Arriaga ©

THE THREE PLAYERS IN A TREND.

Within each stage of the market, there are three actors who play a specific role in the trend and who coexist with each other.

- Consumers. Those who adopt a new habit.
- Brands. Solution generators (products and services).
- Catalysts. Boosters who stimulate the evolution of a trend and accelerate the adoption of a habit or idea in a community.

THE THREE PLAYES IN A TREND

BRAND

CATALYST

CONSUMER

Author Gaby Arriaga ©

These three figures are present in each phase of a trend, acting differently in each phase, we will talk more about each of these later.

MARKET	CONSUMER	CATALYST	BRAND
EARLY MARKET	Early Adopter	Initiator	SCUBA DIVER®
EARLY MASS MARKET	Trendy	Specialized Booster	SURFER®
LATE MASS MARKET	Mass Consumer	Generalist Booster	FOAM®
LAGGARD MARKET	Conservative Consumer	Generalist Booster	BATHER®
			PIÑA COLADA®

Author Gaby Arriaga ©

THE WIND, VALUES AND BELIEFS

Just as the wind generates waves that move the water and all that it contains, there are values and beliefs in society that generate movements in the markets. At first they are barely noticeable, but eventually they burst onto the shore like a wave.

"It is best for pregnant women not to reveal their figure," was a dominant belief for centuries. In November 2014, we at Leonardo1452 finished our report "The Mom of the Future," an investigation into the changes that women in Mexico would experience from then until 2050. We sensed that this belief was beginning to evolve; we saw more women showing their bare growing bellies on social media (emulating that famous 1991 Vanity Fair magazine cover featuring a nude, seven-month pregnant Demi Moore), expressing their attractiveness and willingness to remain beautiful and flirtatious even in pregnancy, and setting aside the tender and immaculate images that are typically associated with motherhood. Celebrities from all over the world were also photographed in this way for their networks or for media outlets, establishing it as a tradition or common practice among many pregnant women.

A change in values acts very similar to the wind, it can blow gently or suddenly, like it does in a crisis, and it can also accelerate, change course or awaken a new trend.

Imagine how the atmosphere of the coast changes when the winds of a hurricane hit. The calm is replaced by drastic changes in temperature, cloudy skies, rain and gusts of wind that cause higher and higher waves at sea, changing the landscape of the beach. In the same way, a market can be disrupted by an abrupt change, as was the case in Mexico with the A-H1N1 (swine flu) pandemic in 2009. From that moment on, we became more conscious of our hygiene, we learned the proper way to sneeze and we relearned the importance of washing our hands. New habits emerged that achieved a change in behavior. For example, antibacterial hand gel is now easily available at the entrance of any building, food centers such as restaurants and cafeterias, and even at many street taco stands. Perhaps this has been an important value in other cultures for some time, but in Mexico it gained relevance after H1N1 pandemic and even more during the COVID pandemic, turning out to be common and almost natural habit.

You can find the video we made in 2009 about the change in values and eventually habits on our YouTube channel: "Trends after Influenza A (H1N1) - Mexico" -

Scan here!

A trend arises from a change in the values or beliefs of a society.

In his book Crossing the Chasm: Marketing and Selling High-Tech Products to Mainstream Customers, Geoffrey Moore, an organizational theorist and business consultant, says that one of the main drivers of a trend is when the early mass market consumer sees a use for the product in his or her daily life. While I totally agree, I insist that it is a change in the values or beliefs of a society that causes the chasm mentioned by G. Moore, and that consumers take not only a new product seriously, but also an idea, to incorporate it into their daily lives.

The key for a trend hunter is to recognize the precise moment when a value or belief changes.

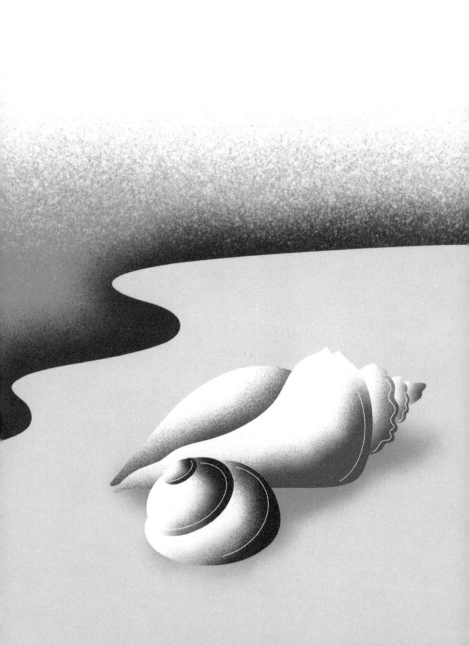

3.THE EARLY MARKET

Just as the wind stirs the waters and causes movement beneath, so begins the interaction between the three players: catalysts, consumers and brands.

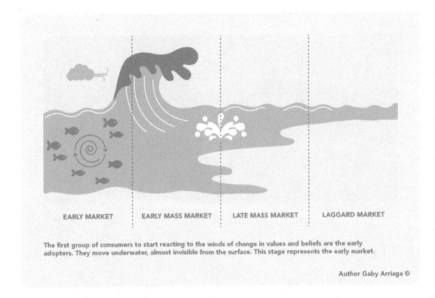

EARLY MARKET   EARLY MASS MARKET   LATE MASS MARKET   LAGGARD MARKET

The first group of consumers to start reacting to the winds of change in values and beliefs are the early adopters. They move underwater, almost invisible from the surface. This stage represents the early market.

Author Gaby Arriaga ©

CATALYSTS OF THE EARLY MARKET: THE INITIATORS

The catalysts, who we will call initiators when they are in the early market, are less influential in terms of diffusion. However, the level of credibility of each catalyst is inversely proportional to their reach, since the stances, messages and opinions of a catalyst in the early market have greater credibility than those who speak to the laggard market.

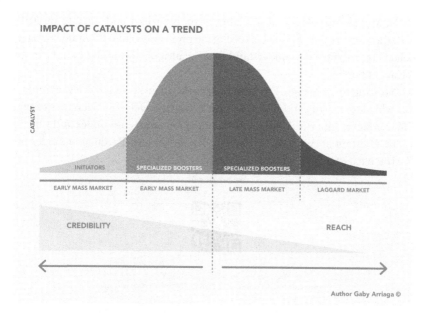

IMPACT OF CATALYSTS ON A TREND

CATALYST

INITIATORS | SPECIALIZED BOOSTERS | SPECIALIZED BOOSTERS

EARLY MASS MARKET | EARLY MASS MARKET | LATE MASS MARKET | LAGGARD MARKET

CREDIBILITY | REACH

Author Gaby Arriaga ©

Initiators are the first to put out an element that makes a trend tangible. These elements can be a manifesto, a work of art or a piece of literature.

Surely you know of business models designed for a society that rents rather than buys, preferring to take a shared trip by car or bike instead of buying a private vehicle; or perhaps splitting a communal space like an office or a house; or renting products and spaces that spend a lot of time in disuse, such as a room in a home that is normally vacant. All of this is part of the much-talked-about Sharing Economy.

In her book All Our Kin, American anthropologist Carol B. Stack writes about how poor and racially segregated families operate as a social network that allows them to meet their needs for survival, such as food and health, by exchanging goods and services. Carol observed how women exchanged bread and vegetables for diapers and milk; others for televisions, cars, cigarettes and even money. The anthropologist realized that these people saw the solutions to their problems in others.

Carol Stack served as an initiator of this trend by publishing her findings in a piece of writing so that more people could learn about it. Putting her ideas out there in a vehicle such as a book made her a catalyst of the sharing trend, which, as the years went by and the markets evolved, became even more sophisticated, as we will see in its early mass market stage.

In Mexico, we identified initiators of the sharing trend starting in 2010 with the launch of the Ecobici bike-sharing program. While this model wasn't born here, we started to understand that the idea of consuming went beyond the act of buying.

Noticing this wave start to form in Mexico, in 2012 we interviewed initiators which we called catalysts of the future: Martha Delgado, Secretary of the Environment; Alberto Padilla and Paloma Corcuera, co-founder and Operations Assistant at Aventones, respectively; and Jimena Pardo, co-founder of Carrot, a car-sharing company in Mexico.

Scan here!

Trend-O-Scope: Sharing Economy Trend
By Leonardo 1452, Featuring some of the initiators in Mexico City.

In 2011, we also saw the birth of the first coworking or shared work space: El 3er Espacio (I) (The Third Space). This startup bet on a business model whereby a space could be equipped with all the amenities of an office for independent professionals (freelancers) or startups to share among themselves.

In an interview with Leonardo1452, the founders were very clear on the benefits of this business model for their members. Not only was it a matter of affordability, but also of being connected to a community and being able to network - at that time, the term networking was still new, in fact, the founders didn't even mention it in the interview - through meeting other professionals, to resolve questions or forge new alliances.

In the video clip, a girl from London talks about the coworking concept. She had already seen such coworking spaces in the United Kingdom, where the wave had risen months before it did in Mexico.

Scan here!

Trend-O-Scope: The Third Space
By Leonardo1452. featuring an interview with the founders of
El 3er Espacio, initiators of the "sharing" trend in Mexico City.

EARLY MARKET CONSUMERS: THE EARLY ADOPTERS

Early adopters and initiators move around in a circle as they react to the wind blowing their way. An initiator survives because an early adopter listens to and agrees with their ideas, or consumes their products and services. Similarly, an early adopter demands the existence of an initiator.

A water current that cannot be seen from the surface, at this point, the trend is only perceptible if you are immersed in it. This stage is known as the early market in the trend adoption curve.

> An Early Adopter's first impulse is not to buy the new thing, but to reflect on their surroundings.

A common myth in business is that an early adopter rushes to a store to buy a new product just because they want to be the first to have it. A true early adopter, however, does so to meet a need that has changed, and their behavior is divided into several stages which can be seen in the following graph.

First, an early adopter changes their values or beliefs, then their priorities, and finally their habits. They begin by questioning whether the world and their surroundings could be different. They are not thinking about consuming, but about beliefs and values. They challenge and question what the rest of the population currently believes.

For example, Salvador, who thinks, "Why buy a car if it's just a shackle in this city?" Or Teresa who muses, "There must be a better way to be able to get the clothes and wardrobe I want at a lower cost. Looking good shouldn't just be for people with money.

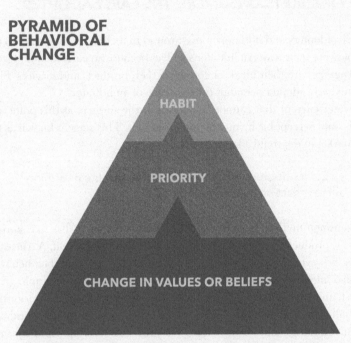

PYRAMID OF BEHAVIORAL CHANGE

HABIT

PRIORITY

CHANGE IN VALUES OR BELIEFS

The behavioral change of an early adopter first starts with a change in their values or beliefs, leading them to adjust their priorities, and finally, their consumer habits.

Author Gaby Arriaga ©

If the early adopter finds other like-minded people, companies or organizations, they will start to change their priorities in terms of consumption. Something the early adopter used to do on a regular basis starts to change. For example, Salvador tries using a bike like Ecobici **(II)** or Econduce **(III)** (the complete range of vehicle lending systems operating in Mexico City), a car sharing platform, or a skateboard at least once a week. Or, Teresa, wondering if she can get a luxury dress for under $1,000 dollars, would surely try a service like Troquer or GoTrendier, which buy and sell second-hand luxury apparel and accessories in Mexico and across Latin America.

These consumers change their priorities when Salvador chooses to ride his bike to work, or when Teresa considers looking for a dress at Troquer before going to buy one at a department store. When these decisions repeat over time, they become a habit; Salvador eventually ends up commuting by bike or skateboard instead of buying a car; and Teresa believes that thrift shopping is smart both for events and her day-to-day life.

Other important aspects to keep in mind about early adopters:

- They are enthusiasts. They love to share their values, discoveries and experiences with others. For example, once they start using Ecobici, they will seek to get more people on board so that they shift their priorities and create a future habit.
- They are drawn to anything new that interests them or falls within their personal set of values. They are willing to pay the price or take the risk of relying on a product or service that might not exist in the future.
- An early adopter is not always an early adopter. Whether or not one is an early adopter depends on the particular tastes of each consumer. For example, a consumer may be an early adopter in the kitchen because they are enthusiastic about experimenting, but not with their closet because they are not as interested in fashion.

They are an ideal candidate for co-creation and testing of new products. If you have an innovative business proposal, it is very likely that your first customers are already your early adopters.

An Early Adopter is not a consumer target, but an innovation target.

UNDERSTANDING THE EARLY MARKET IS CRITICAL

It is in the early market phase where we find clues that a mass market trend is approaching. These clues are hardly noticeable at the beginning. But if you pay close attention to them, in the near future they may become a wave that is too big to ignore.

The early market is essential to identifying a nascent trend.

4. THE EARLY MASS MARKET

We have reached the point where everything going on with the trend is much more visible. Let's leave the underwater world behind and take a surfboard out to where the waves are rising. These waves are surging because they have been carrying energy over a distance for a long time. This moment is the near future; it is imminent that a rising wave will crash on top of everything ahead of it.

In business and in trends, this wave represents a movement that has been building for some time and has gained so much strength, generated by the interaction between early adopters and initiators, that it is no longer a topic of interest to the few, but to the majority. There is no doubt that it will impact the next group of consumers: the trendy ones.

In addition, we are now starting to see a new type of catalyst, the specialized boosters.

EARLY MASS MARKET

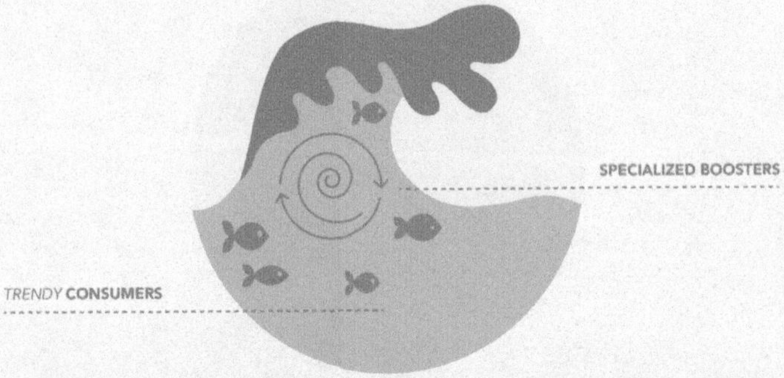

SPECIALIZED BOOSTERS

TRENDY CONSUMERS

The wave is the stage of the trend that is supercharged with activity between specialized boosters and the trendy consumers.

Author Gaby Arriaga ©

CATALYSTS OF THE EARLY MASS MARKET: THE SPECIALIZED BOOSTERS

We call these catalysts the specialized boosters - they have a certain status with their audience because they are most knowledgeable about a particular topic.

Specialized boosters have a wider reach than initiators and a sufficient degree of credibility to have their message be taken seriously by their audience.

TYPES OF BOOSTERS AND THEIR MESSAGING VEHICLES

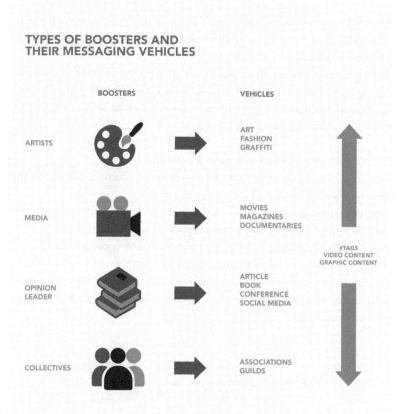

BOOSTERS	VEHICLES
ARTISTS	ART FASHION GRAFFITI
MEDIA	MOVIES MAGAZINES DOCUMENTARIES
	#TAGS VIDEO CONTENT GRAPHIC CONTENT
OPINION LEADER	ARTICLE BOOK CONFERENCE SOCIAL MEDIA
COLLECTIVES	ASSOCIATIONS GUILDS

Boosters can be individuals, a group or even an outlet. The vehicles they utilize to spread a message are vast, ranging from an article of clothing, to a documentary, to a march in the streets. Even digital content such as an amateur video or a series of images linked to a hashtag can be very powerful vehicles to spread a message. Below are just a few examples of the vehicles boosters use.

Author Gaby Arriaga ©

La Lonja MX **(IV)** is a project of Promotora Nacional that seeks to raise awareness of Mexican design and goods. Using a pop-up store concept, La Lonja MX brings together designers and suppliers in a commercial space where they can showcase their creations and sell directly to the general public. This collective acts as a specialized booster of a trend that places even more value on national products than on foreign imports.

EARLY MASS MARKET CONSUMERS: THE TRENDY CONSUMERS

Trendy consumers are those who are aware of the latest thing on the market, thus falling on the left side of the trend adoption curve, but who do not take the same risks as an early adopter.

Trendy consumers are more numerous than early adopters. This is the first group of consumers that attracts a lot of attention from companies. As a company, you can now set aggressive sales targets with these consumers.

Characteristics of a trendy consumer:

- They adopt habits in order to protect their status.
- They need to feel confident that an innovative proposition will stay in the market for a while, that it won't disappear quickly.
- They seek validation from a booster that their decision to adopt a new habit, attend a new venue, or buy a certain product or service is cool.
- They are value-conscious. That is, they expect that the price they pay, whatever the tier, will give them a return that adds points to their status quo.

Aesthetics and design are extremely important to them. They are not interested in a prototype or a test product, qualities that an early adopter might even find fascinating.

A coolhunter is a specialist in the EARLY MASS MARKET and WHAT'S IN FASHION, a trendhunter across the whole trend.

5. MODE

It is very common to confuse the concept of "what's in fashion" with a trend, however, mode is an ephemeral moment. To use the metaphor of the wave, mode is the very moment in which the wave bursts, releasing a tremendous amount of energy which creates an impossible-to-miss explosion. It is the moment when a product or service reaches its highest level of popularity and at the same time, when it begins to decline in novelty.

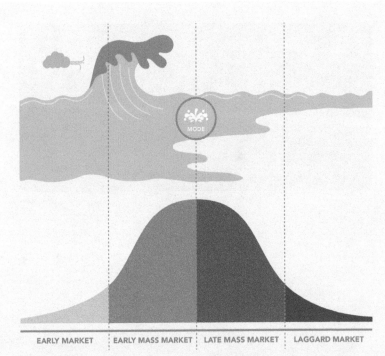

EARLY MARKET | EARLY MASS MARKET | LATE MASS MARKET | LAGGARD MARKET

Mode is the fleeting moment when a product or service reaches its highest level of popularity and at the same time, when it begins to decline in novelty. That moment when the wave breaks and crashes into the sea represents this market phenomenon very well.

Author Gaby Arriaga ©

One example of this are the yellow "Livestrong" bracelets, which were created by Lance Armstrong and Nike in 2004 to bring in revenue and help cancer patients. The bracelets were so successful that, according to Fast Company magazine, up to 100,000 bracelets were sold daily ("How the Lance Armstrong Foundation Became Livestrong,").

Scan here!

How the Lance Armstrong Foundation Became Livestrong

With Livestrong, there were two major triggers behind its success: Lance wore the bracelet while competing in and winning his sixth Tour de France title, as did the Nike-sponsored athletes at the 2004 Olympics in Athens. Both of these situations were boosters that made the accessory so popular.

At the heart of this wave, however, was the new solidarity of society with important causes; giving back was becoming the new status quo. "I like to help and it looks good to help. It looks good to show that I care about others' health or other problems in my community and that I'm involved in the solution." Such was the new way of thinking, a change in beliefs led to the success of these Livestrong bracelets and many more initiatives. Today, posting on social media that you support a positive change in society is seen as a good thing.

MODES

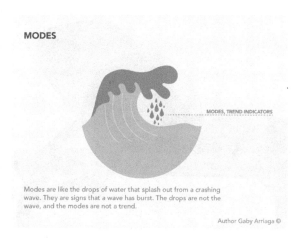

MODES, TREND INDICATORS

Modes are like the drops of water that splash out from a crashing wave. They are signs that a wave has burst. The drops are not the wave, and the modes are not a trend.

Author Gaby Arriaga ©

Behind many latest fashion there is a trend.

6. THE LATE MASS MARKET

Now we are at a point in the wave where its force begins to dissipate. The water gradually begins to wash up on the beach, but still with a little bit of foam. The explosion has passed, and you can feel that the energy in the water is gradually subsiding.

The specialized boosters stop talking and it is the generalist boosters who continue to talk about every new expression of the trend, though the interest of the first two consumer groups decreases.

Many companies wait until this point to launch a product on the market, because if the marketing and communication strategy is right, it's a guarantee that the product will attract a considerable volume of consumers.

In 2018, for a brand in Mexico to launch a product with the ingredient, flavor or smell of coconut meant that they were betting on volume and not on innovation. Several months prior, we at Leonardo1452 observed how this ingredient was increasingly integrated into our daily lives - in beverages, oils, shampoos, and creams - until it became fashionable. By this time, the mass consumer was already buyingproducts containing, tasting or smelling of coconut. Just the simple image of a coconut on the packaging would likely lead the mass consumer to buy the product, without so much as checking the label.

CATALYSTS OF THE LATE MASS MARKET: THE GENERALIST BOOSTERS

A generalist booster covers a variety of topics without any particular expertise. An example is the prime time news anchor who provides important information about everything that happened during the day.

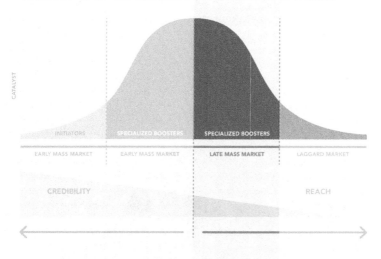

DEGREE OF REACH AND CREDIBILITY OF THE CATALYSTS OF A TREND

CATALYST

INITIATORS · SPECIALIZED BOOSTERS · SPECIALIZED BOOSTERS

EARLY MASS MARKET · EARLY MASS MARKET · LATE MASS MARKET · LAGGARD MARKET

CREDIBILITY · REACH

Generalist boosters use mainstream media to achieve greater reach but less credibility because their messages are varied and superficial.

Author Gaby Arriaga ©

LATE MASS MARKET CONSUMERS: THE MASS CONSUMERS

The primary factors a mass consumer takes into account when choosing a brand are very practical matters such as:

- Price. A mass consumer is very price-sensitive, because they are buying something they have learned from generalist boosters that they must have. They will choose the option that fits their budget over the status quo.
- Proximity. It should be very easy for the mass consumer to find the product or service. It must be embedded in their regular shopping routine.
- Differentiation. The mass consumer will look for the option that provides something unique from the rest of the brands. Not only in price and proximity, but in an added benefit that positively impacts their experience when consuming or using it.

A blockbuster that sells at high volumes is intended for a mass consumer, who is not looking for innovative products, but rather for products that meet a need - at an accessible price point and available at any point of sale, even at the corner store.

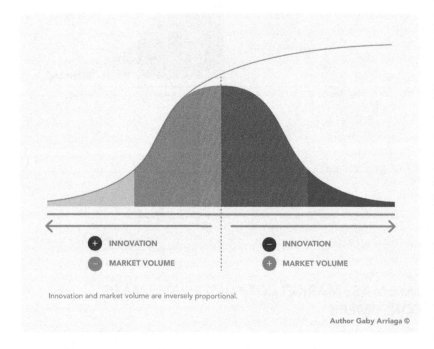

Innovation and market volume are inversely proportional.

Author Gaby Arriaga ©

Everything that happens in the water before the wave breaks is far more fascinating than what happens afterwards, and that has a direct influence on innovation.

7. THE LAGGARD MARKET

We have reached the moment when the water arrives to different areas of the beach, traveling slowly and with limited strength and depth.

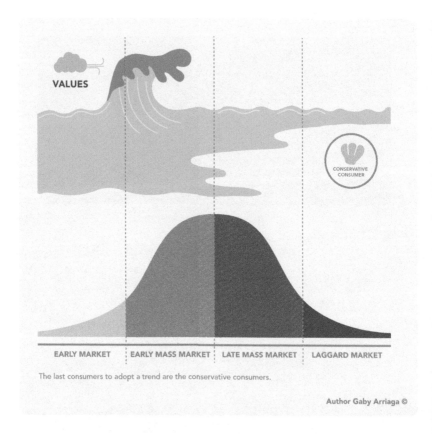

EARLY MARKET ┊ EARLY MASS MARKET ┊ LATE MASS MARKET ┊ LAGGARD MARKET

The last consumers to adopt a trend are the conservative consumers.

Author Gaby Arriaga ©

CATALYSTS OF THE LATE MASS MARKET: THE GENERALIST BOOSTERS ONCE AGAIN

The messages of generalist boosters also reach the ears of conservative consumers, especially if these catalysts use a major media platform that reaches a large audience. Nevertheless, the message may also come from another consumer, perhaps having a greater impact on him or her than the opinion of a journalist. Imagine a consumer who is conservative in terms of environmental stewardship, who, despite constant media coverage of the need to reduce plastics, only changes their daily habits after hearing from an early adopter, trendy or even mass consumer about how bad plastic use is, and who then teaches the conservative consumer how to stop using it.

LAGGARD MARKET CONSUMERS: CONSERVATIVES

These consumers are almost always portrayed as people who are very resistant to change, as if it were an attitude toward life to reject everything new. But at Leonardo1452 we have found that these consumers are slower to adopt a new habit for a variety of reasons:

- Disinterest. For example, if in 2018 a consumer was just barely aware of the term contouring (a makeup technique), then chances are they're either disinterested in the topic or only wear basic makeup.
- Because they favor the "classics." Suppose there are people who, by their own conviction, choose vinyl instead of digital to defend a particular format that is meaningful to them.
- Because they do not see an immediate benefit. To illustrate this idea, think of all the people who are just starting to separate their trash, who had little incentive to do so before or did not see any immediate consequence in their environment.
- Because of misinformation. For example, those consumers who are just starting to shop or make payments using their cell phones but who are still distrustful of this system.
- Limited access to products. Whether due to geographic location or economic resources, a techy is unable to buy a Tesla car if the brand is not present in his country or if buying a Tesla is out of his budget.

One lesson we have learned at Leonardo1452 after years of observing consumer behavior through the lens of trends is that you cannot attach definitive labels. No one is a conservative consumer in every consumer decision they make, nor an early adopter, as much as they might want everything to be new.

A consumer can be conservative in one industry and an early adopter in another. For this reason, stray away from the belief that every early adopter, trendy, mass or conservative consumer is uniquely that profile and always behaves in the same way. We all adopt a different profile according to our personal interests.

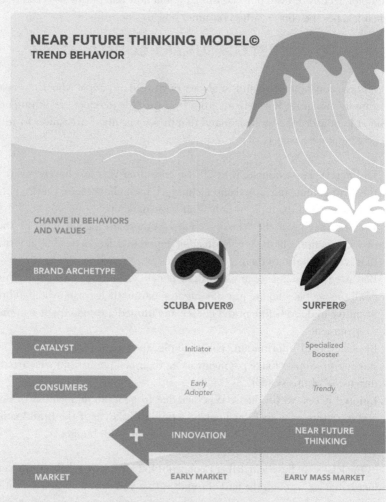

NEAR FUTURE THINKING MODEL©
TREND BEHAVIOR

CHANVE IN BEHAVIORS
AND VALUES

BRAND ARCHETYPE

SCUBA DIVER®

SURFER®

	SCUBA DIVER®	SURFER®
CATALYST	Initiator	Specialized Booster
CONSUMERS	Early Adopter	Trendy
INNOVATION		NEAR FUTURE THINKING
MARKET	EARLY MARKET	EARLY MASS MARKET

A wave in the sea rises, peaks and disappears just like a consumer trend. This depiction shows an consumers, catalysts and brands with the strongest ties to innovation and that set foot in the near behave according to what has worked for them so far.

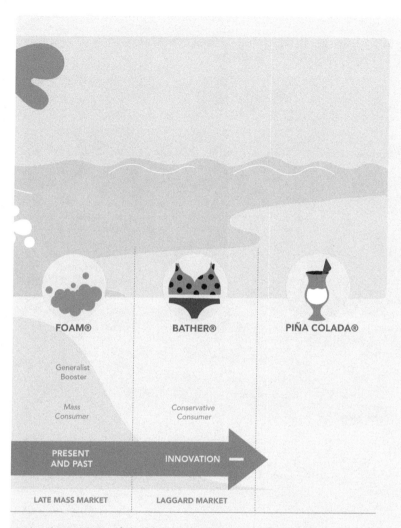

FOAM® BATHER® PIÑA COLADA®

Generalist
Booster

Mass
Consumer

Conservative
Consumer

PRESENT
AND PAST INNOVATION —

LATE MASS MARKET LAGGARD MARKET

organic and pragmatic view of what is happening in the markets. On the left side are the
future before anyone else. On the right side are those who are slower to innovate and

Author: Gaby Arriaga ©

53

SUMMARY OF CONSUMER CHARACTERISTICS
AT EACH STAGE OF A TREND

	EARLY MARKET	EARLY MASS MARKE
TYPE OF CONSUMER	*Early Adopter*	*Trendy*
TIE TO INNOVATION	Very strong ★★★★	Strong ★★★
ATTRACTED BY	New ideas that have the potential to transform their environment.	• New ideas with a commerci. approach. • The status acquired from le. about something new. • Perceived value.
PRICE SENSITIVITY	Low ★	Medium ★★
THEY CHANGE THEIR HABITS...	Because first, they questioned their values and beliefs. Then, they found a Catalyst - Initiator who motivated a change in their priorities and behavior.	• Upon sensing a shift in the v beliefs of certain communiti • To be an avid enthusiast of 1 ing trend.
WHO INFLUENCES THEIR DECISIONS	Catalysts Initiators.	• Specialized Boosters. • Early Adopters.
THEY WILL CHOOSE A BRAND IF	• It continuously provides them with surprises and disruptive solutions. • It makes them feel part of a select group. • In other words, a **SCUBA DIVER®** brand.	• It makes them feel like they newest thing. • Their product does not cat mass consumers too quickly • It gives them the peace of n there won't be too many ch. • In other words, a **SURFER®** brand.

...ET	LAGGARD MARKET	LATE MASS MARKET
	Mass Consumer	Conservative Consumer
	Moderate ★★	Weak ★
...al ...arning	• Having whatever is "in fashion". • Proximity. • Product differentiation.	• That which does not imply a risk. • Products that have been tried out and improve.
	High ★★★	Very high ★★★★
...alues and ...es. ...he grow-	• Because the product or service is very accessible. • Out of imitation and to avoid being left out of the conversation.	• Because their habits are obsolete. • In resignation.
	• Generalist Boosters. • Trendy consumers.	• Generalist Boosters. • Mass consumers.
...have the ...ch on with ...nind that ...anges.	• It is ever-present across all media and mass sales channels, both online and offline. • It does not make frequent changes. • In other words, a **FOAM®** brand.	• It offers them the bare minimum solution at the best price and it is easy to shop for it, pay for it, pick it up and return it if necessary. • They provide them with a simple version of the product. • In other words, a **BATHER®** brand.

Author Gaby Arriaga ©

SUMMARY OF CATALYST CHARACTERISTICS
AT EACH STAGE OF A TREND

	EARLY MARKET	E.
TYPE OF CATALYST	INITIATOR (**TRENDSETTER®**)	SP
REACH	LIMITED ★	N
DEGREE OF CREDIBILITY	HIGH ★★★	
EXAMPLE	• A restless iconoclast. • An early adopter who created a solution that responded to a change in values.	• A journalist particular su • Opinion lea • Coolhunters

Remember that catalysts can have different forms and are present in all marke

ARLY MASS MARKET	LAGGARD MARKET	LATE MASS MARKET
ECIALIZED BOOSTER	GENERALIST BOOSTER	
MODERATE ★★	LARGE ★★★	
MEDIUM ★★	LOW ★	
with expertise in one bject. ders. s.	Mass media providing general news.	

ets. These examples are just for quick reference.

Author Gaby Arriaga ©

8. BRAND ARCHETYPES IN RELATION TO TRENDS

Understanding how a wave forms is fundamental, but if you want to catch one, it's not enough just to know the principles. You have to get into the water.

At Leonardo1452, we have discovered that, as a brand, you can ride all the different points of a trend: at its source, its peak or its decline. Deciding where you want to or should be will depend on your objectives as a brand. Likewise, you can position yourself at the start or at the tail end of a wave. It is very important that you are the one who decides your position and that the wave does not decide your position for you. This decision will depend on the

profile of your company, its mission, its organizational culture or the stance of its leader.

Brand archetypes in relation to trends is the most important contribution of the Near Future Thinking® framework. It is much easier to assimilate each archetype once you have understood the trend adoption curve and its key actors.

BATHER®

PIÑA COLADA®

Λ®

Author Gaby Arriaga ©

SCUBA DIVER® BRAND

A SCUBA DIVER® brand works quietly underwater to explore the unknown - it is the first to detect a change in the ocean.

ITS MOTTO:
"I am going to change the world."

SCUBA DIVER® brands are the most innovative. They are virtually invisible under the water as they work hard to create a disruption in the market. Their targets are the early adopters, since they are the first to respond to changes in values and beliefs. Therefore, these brands are fully aware that they are launching a product or service that responds to a change in values or beliefs in society.

SCUBA DIVER® BRAND

EARLY
ADOPTER
TRENDY
CONSUMER
MASS
CONSUMER
CONSERVATIVE
CONSUMER

EARLY MARKET | EARLY MASS MARKET | LATE MASS MARKET | LAGGARD MARKET

SCUBA DIVER® brands are the most innovative, located at the left most extreme of the trend adoption curve. Relative to the wave, they are underwater, working almost invisibly.

Author Gaby Arriaga ©

Let's talk about their characteristics. A SCUBA DIVER® brand is in constant contact with the early adopters, as they will be the ones to test its products and give them feedback. Or, it will bring its early adopters together so that they can shape the idea of a new product or service. Remember that, as we saw in the chapter "The Early Market," early adopters are an innovation target, not a consumer target.

Does a brand that is born as a SCUBA DIVER® always remain in this archetype? Brands that emerge in the early market are, in principle, a SCUBA DIVER® brand only because they were born in the infancy of a trend, in the depths of the sea. However, like with any brand, it will have to make a decision as to which archetype it wants to be. If it wants to remain a SCUBA DIVER® brand, it should always behave like one, experimenting and adopting more of the attitudes that I will discuss here. SCUBA DIVER® brands can also grow by covering more and more of the market, eventually becoming a BATHER® brand. Once an innovator, this brand has decided to continue offering the same product for many years.

A SCUBA DIVER® brand is aware that it is introducing a product or service that addresses a change in a society's values or beliefs. A SCUBA DIVER® brand does not arise out of the economic need of someone who wants to start a business. Nor does this brand come about as a result of a business idea that, because the timing was right, was quickly adopted. A company that has SCUBA DIVER® brands is also aware that:

A.The volume of the market it serves will be small. Remember that the early market is limited and there are few early adopters. Not only must companies find them, but they must also create them. The users will be few, but they will be very loyal and willing to try your product or service even if it is not yet perfect.

B.Most of your time will be spent experimenting. As a SCUBA DIVER® brand, you will focus on developing products and services that address a change in values and beliefs, not on creating new products with new technologies just for the sake of using them. At first, these products may be rejected, disliked, misunderstood by consumers, or even seen as a mistake, but they are not. The mistake is in thinking that these products must be a sales hit; they will not always achieve this, or at least not at this point in the wave.

Google is a SCUBA DIVER® brand that knows all about experimentation. It launches new products on the market to solve the needs of its users, who determine what improvements should be made, if the product has potential, or if it should die. Some of the products that early technology adopters tried out and did not make it into the hands of trendy consumers were the following:

- GOOGLE WAVE, a platform for teams to collaborate with each other by sharing images, text and links to sites on the Internet. Some say it was difficult to use even for Google employees. The company decided to retire the product just a year after launching it in 2009.
- GOOGLE NOTEBOOK, where users could save miscellaneous notes. Notebook eventually disappeared, and instead, Google created Google Docs, a platform similar to Microsoft Office's Word for creating documents, sharing them with other users, and editing them in real time.

C. The challenge for a SCUBA DIVER® brand is to provide its consumers with continuous news, updates and new products that surprise them. Remember that at this stage, sales are not generated in high volume, but a lot of knowledge is accumulated as a result of continuous experimentation. Once you have a prototype, it is important to test it on early adopters to get immediate feedback. There is no need to wait for the product to be in perfect condition in terms of design or materials, nor for it to be priced according to the value of its benefit. In fact, to achieve all of the above, you will need a mature market. At this moment, that is, before the wave is formed, the market is still very young. Remember that you will keep your early adopters close as long as you awaken their excitement to try something new.

In 2014, Google launched Inbox, a new platform for managing emails that would be more efficient than their own Gmail. As they said on their website: "Taking into account what we've learned from Gmail, Inbox is a fresh start that goes beyond email, to let you focus on what really matters." Inbox started out as an invite-only product (a well executed strategy to make early adopters feel special), but later anyone could use it, including me. One day, while writing this book, I received a notification that Inbox would be discontinued in a few months. The message read "Gmail Inbox is going away at the end of March 2019. The new Gmail has a refreshed look that builds on Inbox features like reminders and more to help you be more productive."

Naturally, I was sorry to hear the news because I had already gotten used to Inbox and had found it to have very practical features that other email services did not offer. However, I enjoyed the experience of trying a new product from a brand I like and I left the service knowing that in the near future I would see something from Inbox integrated into Gmail, and that Google would surprise me with other news soon.

D.You must be prepared to receive negative feedback from users who are upset because they don't like your product. With so much exposure to feedback from your users, you must be willing to listen to both good and bad opinions, especially the bad ones, because those are the ones that will get your product across the chasm. So, you'll need tough skin if you're a SCUBA DIVER® brand.

E.You will be less likely to gain exposure in the mainstream media, as outlets will only become interested when your impact on the market is greatest (that of a SCUBA DIVER® brand is minimal in terms of volume). It is more likely that media specialized in your industry will be the ones to cover your every move.

More examples of SCUBA DIVER® brands:

Have you ever attended a FUCKUP NIGHTS **(VI)** event? If you have, you are witnessing a Mexican SCUBA DIVER® brand. Fuckup Nights are events that consist of different speakers who recount their business failures to an unfamiliar audience. In the words of the founders, Fuckup Nights revolve around: "Stories of businesses that go bust and catch fire, sponsorships that end badly, products that have to be recalled... We tell all of those stories":

Scan Here!

Fuckup Nights are now organized in other cities across the Americas, Europe, Africa, Asia and the Middle East. The brand started the conversation about failure in our country and did so with great difficulty, like a good SCUBA DIVER® brand.

Co-founder Pepe Villatoro says: "In the early days of Fuckup Nights, it wasn't cool to be us. We were like a pest. It wasn't cool to put Fuckup Nights on your LinkedIn profile, sharing your failures was a sign of weakness, and some of our friends even avoided us, afraid that we would ask them to be speakers. We were those masochistic freaks who liked to hear stories of failure. And no one wanted to have any kind of contact with us. A former partner even suggested to me that his coworking space shouldn't be associated with Fuckup Nights - a space we both founded! Then, like many things, it all started to take off. We found our audience. We found a community. We became a little bit cooler (for a small group of hipsters and creators in Mexico City)":

Scan Here!

Nowadays, Fuckup Nights isn't only for telling stories of losses and defeats, but a complete business model that includes Fuckup Knowledge, a research area aimed at improving decision making in business, education and public policy, thanks to the large number of case studies accumulated over the years. Do you see the importance of user feedback for a SCUBA DIVER® brand? Some of their studies include "The Impact of Digital Skills on Entrepreneurship" and "Low-income Women Entrepreneurs: Failure and Empowerment."

One of the founders, Leticia Gasca, published the book Sobrevivir el fracaso (Surviving Failure), which undoubtedly works as a booster of this trend. By encouraging more people and companies to consider this view of failure, they may eventually change their perspective and see it as a tool for growth.

A SCUBA DIVER® Brand is for you if you are willing to invest in the development and testing of new products and services on an ongoing basis.

SCUBA DIVER® BRAND

POSITION ON THE WAVE   Before it forms

TYPE OF CONSUMER

Early Adopters

SHARE OF MARKET VOLUME

★ **Not much** volume but loyal clients who are willing to try your product even before it's finished.

LIFETIME

★★★★★ You'll have lots of time to experiment, seek feedback and make changes to your prototype.

LEVEL OF EXPOSURE

★ **Not much**. Remember that you are underneath the water. But you can get exposure from specialized media outlets and your early adopters.

THIS BRAND IS IDEAL FOR YOU IF...

- You're willing to invest in research and development of new products.

- You will provide the resources for your company to develop disruptive ideas.

- You have the capacity to test and implement ideas.

- Your company is open to criticism, especially negative criticism.

- Your organizational culture is geared toward innovation and encouraged to innovate by your higher-ups.

EXAMPLE BRANDS   Google, Fuckup Nights

Author Gaby Arriaga ©

SURFER® BRAND

A SURFER® brand knows how to position itself at the right moment of the wave and ride it. It must keep its balance and be ready for the next one.

ITS MOTTO:
"I am the one who will massify a new trend."

SURFER® brands are right on top of the wave, serving a trendy consumer just when the trend has already taken shape. At this point, consumers have started to change their values, priorities and habits. The brand is no longer in a trial period. Now, it's in the spotlight, with lots of eyes watching their every move.

SURFER® BRAND

The type of market that **SURFER®** brands cater to is primarily the early mass market. They are in a spot, like surfers, where they have the attention of everyone on the beach, that is, everyone who participates in any type of market, from the early to the laggard.

Author Gaby Arriaga ©

SURFER® brands are the ones tasked with massifying a trend or product that responds to a change in values and beliefs. They are the first to offer their branded solution to the trendy and mass consumers, a larger market segment in terms of volume.

To be a SURFER® brand is to be right at the point where the wave forms. Just like surfers, these brands ride and stay with the wave for those precious seconds in which it rolls majestically along, staying afloat for as long as possible before the wave crashes and loses its energy. This is a transitional phase in the markets that marks the moment at which a trend goes from being only for a few to being for the majority or mass markets. While the SCUBA DIVER® brands were the first to react to a forthcoming change in values with a new product, service, movement, organization, and so forth, their consumers were exclusively the early adopters. The SURFER® brands, on the other hand, are the first to offer their branded solution to the trendy and mass consumers, a larger market segment in terms of volume. Therefore, the SURFER® brands are the ones tasked with massifying a trend or product that responds to a tangible change in values and beliefs.

Remember that the trendy consumer does not want to buy an experiment, but wants products and services that fulfill a need while adding points to their own status quo. To achieve this, a SURFER® brand must be willing to invest in the following elements:

- **Design**. I see design as the most important element. Bringing a product to the masses is about more than just betting on a larger market volume. It's about preparing a product to be desired and adopted by a large number of people. Not only is this a matter of aesthetics, but of creating a product or service so easy, intuitive and comfortable for the consumer to use that they are able to use it without an instruction manual or industry-specific expertise. Above all, it is imperative that the product invites the consumer to try it right away.

  In my view, one of the reasons why virtual reality has not yet managed to cross the chasm and enter most households is that it is still very uncomfortable to use. For example, VR does not yet integrate with the body as well as wearables (mainly smartwatches) do. When products are friendly to use in our daily lives, then it is significantly easier for us to use them. No one needs to explain the product to us - we use it intuitively, just as a child uses a tablet or a smartphone.

  In Mexico, SÍCLO (**V**) was the very first high-intensity spinning studio, founded by Alejandro Ramos and Pedro de Garay in 2015. To bring it to life, they called up designer Ignacio Cadena and architect Michel Rojkind, both Mexican. This was a very wise decision; the founders knew that the design of the space, the environment and the branding in general was fundamental to the success of this brand. While there are other indoor cycling facilities in Mexico, SÍCLO is a clear example of a brand that brought health and wellness to the early mass market consumer with a hard-to-resist, ready-to-use service.

I believe design is what adds the most status points for a trendy consumer, a consumer who wants to be surrounded by items, spaces and propositions that have carefully crafted aesthetics.

- **Shareability**. We must always keep in mind that the trendy consumer wants to be the one to communicate new information to the mass consumer. Therefore, it must be easy to explain, simple to understand and must invite the consumer to try the product.

Augmented reality, like facial recognition, is an ever-improving technology. One of the early glimpses into its mainstream use was the introduction of filters on the multimedia messaging app Snapchat, featuring a famous rainbow pukingvomit filter that was all the rage back in 2015. Still, many users most likely have no idea that the filters they use on digital platforms are actually a type of augmented reality, as this is not important to them. We can leave the technical details to technology enthusiasts, the early adopters of augmented reality. The most important thing in the eyes of a trendy consumer is that the product is fun, encouraging the user to use and share it with their network of contacts. Shareability is a major tool for massification, provided in this century thanks to the Internet. The social component of digital platforms means that new ideas and their various applications can travel faster than they did in the last century. The ability to share gives life to a community of early mass market users who will consistently use the product or service and who can even suggest new uses for it, much like early adopters. Consider the many ways people use filters to share photos or videos on social media.

- **Value**. This doesn't mean you have to be cheap, but you must deliver the appropriate perceived value. We discussed this back in the chapter "The Early Mass Market." Your trendy consumer must feel that they are paying for the benefit that your product promises, some novelty and exclusivity (but not at the level of early adopters), as well as a design that makes them feel trendy in front of mass consumers.

In 2018, Rihanna launched her lingerie line named SAVAGE X FENTY. Not only is this brand valuable for the artist's endorsement or the raw materials, but it is also valuable for "celebrating courage, confidence and inclusivity." "Savage X is about respect. Do whatever you want. No regrets. Embrace your individuality":

Scan Here!

At Leonardo1452, we analyzed SAVAGE X FENTY to substantiate a trend called "Beauty Emancipation" which is anchored in the belief that all bodies are beautiful. Listen to our podcast to understand it further

Scan Here!

BENEFIT + NOVELTY AND EXCLUSIVITY + DESIGN = PERCEIVED VALUE FOR THE TRENDY CONSUMER.

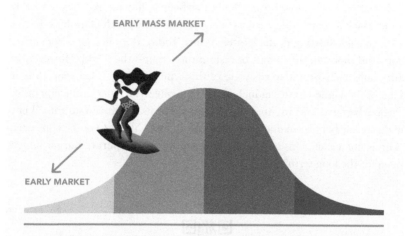

Just as a surfer must use all of their experience to stay afloat while balancing between gravity and buoyancy, a **SURFER®** brand must maintain a balance between the early market and the early mass market.

Author Gaby Arriaga ©

For a few years now, Burger King has been behaving like a SURFER® brand. Back in 2019, it decided to bring burgers made with plant-based meat to the masses, starting in the United States. Today, this offering is appearing more and more on the menus of restaurants around the world. However, in 2019, only a few people were aware of this type of burger. That year, Burger King in the United States launched its Impossible Whopper in the city of St. Louis, Missouri, and in August, nationwide at its 7,200 restaurants. They made a clear bet on volume, as confirmed by Jose Cil, CEO of the company: "This is not a joke. This is something we believe can be part of Burger King's menu for the long term":

Scan Here!

This new meat-like burger is supplied to Burger King by the SCUBA DIVER® brand Impossible. This company's raison d'être is evidence of a change in values. They believe in the value of plant-based "meat," which has a lower impact on the environment than meat from animals.

Surely early adopters of plant-based meat already existed. But now, because society's values have changed, people are generally more planet-conscious. For this reason, a SCUBA DIVER® brand like Impossible invested in the research and development of a more palatable product for mass consumers. Burger King, a mass market brand, was then tasked with bringing this type of food to the majority, presenting it like a regular burger and selling it at a price that its users are willing to pay, making it a SURFER® brand.

It is important to emphasize that for a brand to wear the DIVER® or SURFER® suit, it must make constant efforts to innovate. Just one innovation is not enough. In the case of Burger King, the brand's efforts in the United States to stand out from its competitors in terms of novelty are notorious. One example of this is its past launch of the Dogpper, a dog snack that responded to the new value on pets as members of the family.

In terms of media exposure, the SURFER® brands, unlike the SCUBA DIVER® brands, will get the spotlight because they are noticeable across a larger market. Expect a lot of chatter, media noise, and even naysayers questioning what you're doing, albeit less harshly than with the SCUBA DIVER® brands that are out there making waves in the market. Early adopters with greater knowledge of the product category and niche media may claim that you are not offering anything new, while for the mass and conservative consumers, you are offering a high price tag that is "just for show".

Mass media outlets and those covering general interest topics will approach you to learn more about your products and services, and about how your idea got started. You'll have plenty of unpaid publicity and exposure that will set the bar high, and many will see you as the most innovative brand on the market. Plus, if you get specialized boosters to reassure the trendy consumer, you'll attract even more attention.

To them, you will be perceived as the coolest, most innovative brand. Yes, it is the SURFER® brands in particular that get the "cool" label. The coolhunting media will be on the hunt for SURFER® brands to recommend them to their followers.

Being a SURFER® brand implies a lot of work, because it is not often that you ride the wave at the right time. In fact, being at the right place at the right time is more a matter of work and study than of luck or budget. A SURFER® brand dictates its own momentum. They successfully detect a change in society's values and beliefs, either by their experience in the early market, or by careful observation of what the SCUBA DIVER® brands were creating and the reactions of their early adopters. Then, they improve the three elements we have previously mentioned: design, shareability and perceived value of their products or services, in order to take them to the early mass market.

All of this is hard enough, and to add to it, like a surfer riding a wave, a SURFER® brand's moment of glory - grabbing the attention of the public and the media and being perceived as an innovative brand - is getting shorter and shorter. If the brand is successful, they quickly move on to the next stages: the "in fashion" and late mass markets. There, they will increase their sales, but they also run the risk of losing their innovative edge. To stay on the wave, they must then be able to re-enter the market with another product or service.

Apple, for example, looked not only at what the SCUBA DIVER® brands were doing, but at past products such as the Walkman, which it reconfigured in the form of an iPod to make it cool, a classic move by a SURFER® brand.

So, check if at the moment you are reading this chapter, the brands mentioned here are still SURFER® brands. For these brands to continue on the wave, they must constantly be on the lookout for new changes in values or beliefs and ready to "pirouette" with another product or evolution of a product they have already launched.

On our YouTube channel you will find an interview we did with a surfer, in which he tells us how he rides a wave. Notice the similarities with what happens with trends.

Scan Here!

Tips for Being a Surfer Brand

SURFER® BRAND

POSITION ON THE WAVE	At the top

TYPE OF CONSUMER

Trendy

SHARE OF MARKET VOLUME

★★★ You'll be the first to see high volume. The early mass market consumer will go with you to look cool.

LIFETIME

★★★ You'll have less time than a **SCUBA DIVER®** brand. This moment is like stepping out on a stage to perform a musical you have rehearsed for months. If you're successful, you'll stay afloat throughout the life of this wave, but you must be able to surf the next ones. Whether that's another trend, another product or the evolution of the current product.

LEVEL OF EXPOSURE

★★★★★ **High**. The spotlight's on you. Expect to have many conversations with consumers and a lot of media buzz. So, remember to take very good care of your image, including the statements made by executives and your customer service.

THIS BRAND IS IDEAL FOR YOU IF...

• You have perfected the design, perceived value, and shareability of your product or service.

• You have the ability to balance being innovative with being attractive, while at the same time accessible to the early mainstream.

• You constantly monitor the **SCUBA DIVER®** brands, studying both their successes and failures in the process of experimenting.

• You also investigate past products in the interest of reconfiguring or reintroducing them.

EXAMPLE BRANDS

Savage x Fenty, Burger King, Síclo.

FOAM® BRAND

A FOAM® brand inserts itself at the height of the wave's turmoil. It enjoys the commotion even though it knows it will only be there for a short time.

ITS MOTTO:
"I want to be part of what's in fashion even if it's short-lived."

The FOAM® brands position themselves at the moment a trend becomes fashionable, staying around until the trend begins to lose strength, but before the laggard market becomes interested in it. In relation to the wave, this is the moment when the wave bursts, releasing its energy in a thunderous explosion. Soon after, this phase is replaced by roaring ripples that shake up whatever is still in the water, but which will eventually begin to subside.

FOAM® BRAND

The **FOAM®** brands are at the height of a trend's popularity, when everyone is talking about them. They are now on the right side of the curve, where there is less innovation.

Author Gaby Arriaga ©

It is important to keep in mind that by jumping onboard the fashion of the moment, you are a FOAM® and not a SURFER® brand, since you are betting on fame as opposed to coolness. A FOAM® brand plays it safe - it doesn't try to teach its consumers a new habit, but rather gives them what they want to have in their hands right now.

I remember some examples of trendy moments such as selfies in 2014, fidget spinners (toys made up of three circles that you spun to relieve the anxiety of the day) in 2017, or the countless social media challenges such as the #mannequinchallenge or #whatthefluff.

This is a delicate position, as it seems easy and tempting to get into consumers' daily lives and conversations almost immediately. This position makes it seem like there's not much to investigate in the market and that it's just a matter of joining in with what everyone else is doing. For this very reason, however, there is a lot of turbulence, since, as we saw in the corresponding chapter, the media, companies with high sales targets, opinion leaders and mass consumers will all want to be part of what's "in vogue."

If you decide to be a FOAM® brand, you must take into account that:

- YOU SPEAK TO THE MASS CONSUMERS, who are people with impulse buying tendencies and who at first will pay anything to have that spinner, for example. But as soon as they see more options on the market, that impulse decision will be based on price.
- YES, YOU WILL SUCCEED because you are no longer trying to train consumers on a new habit; early adopters and trendy consumers as well as specialized and generalist boosters will have carved that path. Still, you will have to work hard on other aspects of your brand and product, like the ones I'm describing here.
- YOU MUST STRIVE FOR MASS DIFFUSION since many other FOAM® brands will be seeking the exact same thing (remember the S shape of the trend adoption curve). This is perhaps the area where you will have the most competition, especially in terms of attention, as it will be divided among many media outlets and brands that will talk and present their offerings.

- YOU MUST LOOK FOR WAYS TO DIFFERENTIATE YOURSELF. Imagine that your consumer is a city dweller who takes the to a weekend destination, they stop for a snack on the road in a place with a food stalls plethora. As soon as he steps out of the car he will hear a crowd of people all shouting at the same time: "Come on in, young man, we have squash blossom quesadillas, mushroom quesadillas, tinga quesadillas, pressed pork rind quesadillas, come on in, come on in...". All options sound the same - the traveler gets stunned for a few seconds before going with the salesperson who was able to hold his attention, who shouted louder or who changed something about their message; perhaps by mentioning that all ingredients are homemade or prepared using a special house recipe. FOAM® brands are those Tres Marias salespeople: they all have a chance to sell, but they have to shout a lot and very loudly, requiring a large investment in marketing and unique messaging. All of this in the shortest amount of time possible. If you fail to find something that distinguishes you, you will be seen as a copy, just another option.

New coworking spaces today must differentiate themselves, because here in Mexico City you can find them everywhere, including inside:

- Fitness centers like Load:

Scan here!

- Retailers like OfficeMax stores with Net@Works:

Scan Here!

- Banks like Santander with Work/Café. This video presents the space when it was first launched in Chile:

Scan here!

- Meditation centers.

Many businesses that have physical points of sale or a space where they can welcome their customers have seized the opportunity to leverage their square footage to generate more revenue. I think it's great since this is a retail trend in itself, to juice all of your space. However, with the coworking concept, you must find a way to be different and add value, because even if it seems like a safe business prospect, you could go unnoticed in the midst of so many offerings.

- BEING A FOAM® BRAND IS IDEAL FOR THOSE WHO ARE VERY QUICK to get out into the market while they gear up for the FOAM® that will follow the next new wave. Some examples of FOAM® brands are character licensing brands, such as Disney. These are FOAM® brands that, unlike a media outlet, are completely in control of their own buzz. They produce stories and characters that they can pitch to the media and the public in order to become the topic of conversation. They know that they must be successful content generators that are always in fashion and always desirable for promotional articles, video games, digital content, etc., even if only for a certain period of time.
- REMEMBER THAT BEHIND MANY MODES THERE IS A TREND. I emphasize this because being an FOAM® brand appears to be more about tactics than strategy. However, you must be clear on which trend or wave that FOAM® is coming from, especially if you decide to be FOAM® via a product and not via marketing. For example, you should be well aware of the wellness trend behind beverage X that became fashionable in order for you as a company to launch a different beverage that stands out from the rest, or to create another product or service that is neither beverage nor food, but that responds to the same trend and also becomes fashionable.

Recently, I went to eat at the restaurant Te Quiero Quinoa (I Love You Quinoa). As you can imagine, the dishes are primarily made with quinoa. Does it make sense that there is now a brand based around this ingredient? Of course it does, thanks to new health and wellness habits. However, quinoa is not a trend per se, but rather an expression of the trend towards a healthier lifestyle. This wave brings with it foods such as quinoa, matcha, and turmeric, as well as other expressions such as beauty routines, forms of exercise and even ways of thinking that build on this mega wave sweeping Mexico and the whole world. To bet on a business with "quinoa" in its name strikes me as a bit risky if the ingredient is newly "in fashion," as it could quickly go out of fashion, become old-fashioned, suffer a crisis of attacks from specialists, or be replaced by a new ingredient.

Fast-fashion brands are good examples of FOAM® brands. It is no coincidence that the textile industry embraces the term fashion, since most of the proposed designs have a determined lifespan and will be "out of fashion" in only a few months.

It is very important to keep in mind that if you are a FOAM® brand, act as such. If you consider yourself a SURFER® brand riding the wave of the trend, but in reality you are only out there when the wave has burst, you are hung up on what's "in fashion." You will feel that your budget is not enough, that it is difficult to innovate and that you are always one step behind.

A FOAM ® brand is embedded in fashions and swims in the late mass market, a safe but highly competitive place.

FOAM® BRAND

POSITION ON THE WAVE   In the turbulent water after a wave crashes.

TYPE OF CONSUMER

Mass Consumer

The type of consumer who buys when they find a brand that provides a benefit at a reasonable price.

SHARE OF MARKET VOLUME   ★★★★★ **High**. The massification and market opportunity is evident.

LIFETIME   ★★★ **High**, but only if you focus on trends rather than what's in fashion, and if you find a way to stand out from the competitors.

LEVEL OF EXPOSURE   ★★★★★ **High**. You're in the most scandalous point of the wave. As such, many **FOAM®** brands will gain exposure and you'll need to be creative in order to get noticed.

THIS BRAND IS IDEAL FOR YOU IF...

- You are a brand that plays it safe.

- You prefer to wait until the majority of your consumers have changed their values and habits so that you don't have to train them.

- Your company is oriented toward volume and averse to risk.

- You're a brand with a proven track record that quickly attracts attention.

- You're willing to invest in publicity.

EXAMPLE BRANDS   Coworking spaces after 2018.

Author Gaby Arriaga ©

BATHER® BRAND

A BATHER® brand splashes in the water but does not go too far out to sea.

ITS MOTTO:
"I'm late to the trend, but I'm here."

A BATHER® brand caters to a conservative consumer. This is a stage where the trend, like a wave, has lost its energy to attract the consumers who are excited about innovation. Your audience will be a more conservative consumer who is resistant to change.

BATHER® BRAND

EARLY
ADOPTER / TRENDY CONSUMER / MASS CONSUMER / CONSERVATIVE CONSUMER

EARLY MARKET | EARLY MASS MARKET | LATE MASS MARKET | LAGGARD MARKET

BATHER® brands are at the point where the trend has now matured and will gradually begin to lose steam. It is a safe place because the brand will find undemanding consumers, but at the same time, it will find a lot of competition.

Author Gaby Arriaga ©

The name bather explains its position in relation to the wave. This is the figure of a person who stands facing the ocean after the foam of a wave has receded and the water has washed up on the shore. A bather lets the water wet their feet without much risk while they watch the waves in the distance. Here it doesn't matter if they can't ride a wave, they enjoy just splashing in the water. In the same way, BATHER® brands don't need the experience of a SCUBA DIVER® or SURFER® brand to get in at the early stages of a trend; they can position themselves in the later stages of a trend and be there more comfortably.

For example, in a wave driven by a value such as caring for the environment, a retailer may decide to change its plastic bags for cloth ones. Although it is moving with the trend, a move like this today is not innovative at all because the momentum for it has already passed. This BATHER® brand may innovate with other types of solutions, but not with a cloth bag that all brands, not just retailers, use as merchandising.

More examples of BATHER® brands in Mexico are those brands that waited (on purpose or out of ignorance) until 2020 or later to portray same-sex families in their audiovisual content, such as advertising campaigns or video stories. These brands are doing well - they aren't telling any lies. While it is true that there is a growing number of families headed by two men or two women, in terms of innovation or Near Future Thinking®, these brands are not delivering disruption. Instead, they are "late but here," since this is a widely recognized and accepted reality among mass and conservative consumers. They are sending a message that even their audiences were already expecting.

Being a BATHER suits brands that are committed to launching products, services, content, movements, etc., with very aggressive sales targets. Or brands that do not want to link the reputation of the brand or the company with disruptive movements. This position is also ideal for brands new to understanding consumer trends in their industry. It's like being a surfing apprentice who doesn't plan on catching a wave the first time. A newbie, who doesn't normally ride the waves or innovate, can hang back on the shore, in a safe place, while they observe the others. For example, making the decision to switch from plastic bags to cloth bags in your store or, in the middle of 2019, flying the LGBTI flag on your storefront for Pride month in June. In other words, instead of innovating and making profound changes in your company to demonstrate your change in values, you're reacting after crucial moments have already passed. But at least you have your eyes on the sea, attentive to "what's in fashion" and where the waves are breaking. You are fully aware that you are waiting for the moment when you have gained the experience to be able to enter the water and eventually become a FOAM®, a SURFER® or even a SCUBA DIVER® brand.

I know of very few companies that would proudly acknowledge being a BATHER® brand, catering to the laggard market. Just as being a consumer in this group can be a very smart decision, so too is being a BATHER® brand. There is nothing wrong with deciding to be a more conservative company with regard to innovation, as long as the company embraces its archetype and does not pretend, with its customers and employees, to be perceived as a SURFER® or SCUBA DIVER® brand. Doing so will only create a lot of frustration and hard times. Take for example a person who does not know how to swim but endlessly repeats to himself and his friends that he is an expert on the surfboard.

One thing to definitely avoid is ending up a BATHER® because you ignored the wave, got tossed around, and now you're scraped up on the beach with sand in your ears. If that's the case and you're not a BATHER® because you decided to be, you now need to think about what kind of brand you do want to be. If you are a BATHER® brand, you should keep the following in mind:

- YOUR AUDIENCE WILL BE THE CONSERVATIVE CONSUMERS. This is a significant segment, which is why many brands remain in this position. In addition, their demands are not very high; these consumers are looking for products that solve a need to which they attach little importance. For example, if a consumer is conservative when it comes to nutrition and health, they will only seek a brand that, in addition to tasting good, offers an ingredient that they already know about and understand, such as calcium, a vitamin, iron, a product low in sugar or salt, etc.
- UNLIKE THE FOAM® brands, where dissemination and differentiation are both relevant, in this case the latter will be more important, since there will be more and more competition and prices will be even more accessible than they were during the trend's stage.
- For example, today, a brand that organizes a race in Mexico City is definitely a BATHER® brand, since this is not at all a new activity (in 2014 alone there were 85 options for runners, including races, marathons and half marathons, according to Milenio newspaper, that is, more than one per week!). This activity is no longer innovative either. So, brands seek to differentiate themselves with races run in heels, races where every three kilome-

ters you listen to a different type of music, races where you are greeted with hot chocolate, fondues and sweets when you reach the finish line, or those races that shower you with colored powders. This is when many BATH-ER® brands resort to the appeal of emotional benefits, such as security, happiness, harmony, empowerment, nostalgia, etc., to give their products a unique meaning and position in the eyes of their consumers.

- **THE CONTROL IS NOT YOURS**, but rather, in the hands of the market. You may think you are in safe territory because you now feature same-gender couples or your brand encourages a healthy or eco-friendly lifestyle by promoting a race or reusable bags. But soon another wave will come along with another current and you will have to be prepared for it as well. You can't get too complacent or you'll move on to the next type of brand: the PIÑA COLADA® brand.

Being a BATHER® brand suits companies that are slow to detect changes in their industry, that don't have a Near Future Thinking®, trendhunting or foresight area, that don't invest in innovation, are late to develop a product, or that are sales-oriented rather than disruptive. This archetype, I repeat, should not be seen as negative, but should be honestly assumed as such. Nevertheless, BATHERS® must always be attentive to what FOAM® brands are doing so they can improve their proposal in terms of price and differentiation and launch it to the laggard market.

These brands must always be attentive to what FOAM® brands are doing so they can improve their proposal in terms of price and differentiation and launch it to the laggard market.

BATHER® BRAND

POSITION ON THE WAVE

Some time after the wave has crashed, where the water is shallow and less agitated.

TYPE OF CONSUMER

Conservative Consumers

Your group of consumers isn't looking for a market revolution, but what is tried, improved and accessible.

SHARE OF MARKET VOLUME

★★★★ There is considerable volume of consumers who are ready to buy, but only when they see a clear benefit at a great price.

LIFETIME

(★★) This depends less on you and more on the time it takes for the next powerful wave to arrive.

LEVEL OF EXPOSURE

★ Low. You're one of many and you'll need to find a way to differentiate yourself.

THIS BRAND IS IDEAL FOR YOU IF...

- You want to launch a low-risk product or service that requires very little investment in explanations and tutorials.

- You're slow to innovate.

- You have the capacity to add value to your proposal.

- You want to bring a classic version to the conservative consumers.

EXAMPLE BRANDS

Running races in cities, eco-friendly products.

Author Gaby Arriaga ©

PIÑA COLADA® BRAND

A PIÑA COLADA® brand is comfortably enjoying the beach vibe. It doesn't care about anything that happens in the water.

ITS MOTTO:
"If you snooze, you lose."

PIÑA COLADA® BRAND

PIÑA COLADA® brands are beyond the trajectory of a trend in a position where it is too late to react.

We have reached the last brand archetype, the PIÑA COLADA®. This brand is outside the trend adoption curve, as the trend has already seen its whole cycle: birth, development, zenith, decline and death. This brand is unaware that the trend even existed, and finds itself without consumers to turn to.

It might sound tempting to be a PIÑA COLADA® and I named it that way on purpose; it's far away from the sea, in the privacy and comfort of a palm hut. However, I don't recommend this archetype at all. A PIÑA COLADA® brand is relaxing on the beach, enjoying the warmth with its eyes on the sea, but oblivious to what's going on out in the water. This brand is at the beach bar drinking a cocktail in blissful relaxation. They fail to notice a change in the tide or the swell.

The PIÑA COLADA® brand is happy to keep selling its products and services and is completely unaware of anything happening in its industry. It only notices when everything has changed. While enjoying their piña colada, they are swept away by a giant wave, or even a tsunami, that destroys their peaceful environment and sweeps away everything around them.

Let's think back to traditional television, the TV we used to turn on to tune in to a channel and watch the programming the network decided we should watch, at the time they wanted us to watch it. Broadcast networks and video rental chains like Blockbuster were jolted by the new streaming services of on-demand content from Netflix, Disney, Amazon, Hulu and HBO, TV content on YouTube, and many others, as well as users' own content.

The same thing happened to the music industry, which saw its profits decline from $14.6 billion in 1999 to $6.3 billion in 2009 according to research firm Forrester. This happened once we as users realized that we could download music, first illegally, and listen to it without paying a penny.

It's actually fair to say that the Internet took traditional media and virtually the entire planet by surprise. It was the SCUBA DIVER® brands that were shaped by the hand of the Internet - literally shaped by it - and that would eventually become the SURFER® brands out on the waves.

However, waves keep on coming and whipping up brands. For example, the automotive industry. This industry was quite comfortable believing that the only thing it had to worry about was making cars more or less bulky, more or less comfortable, more or less luxurious, more or less sporty, and more or less expensive. Suddenly, this industry was jolted due to a change in society's values and beliefs. For a segment of consumers, it is no longer attractive to own a car; in fact, for these consumers, a car is just an expense that depletes their economic resources. And those who had a car are getting rid of them, preferring the now numerous reliable and even fun means of transportation such as bicycles or motorcycles, readily available in megacities at an affordable price for everyone.

Today we see the major car brands doing pirouettes in order to float and demonstrate that owning a car is still attractive and necessary. Their solution is to become a center for the development of smarter and more sustainable mobility. And this is all to avoid becoming a PIÑA COLADA® brand, swept away by the tsunami of changes in the automotive industry.

PIÑA COLADA® BRAND

POSITION ON THE WAVE   It doesn't even know where it is.

TYPE OF CONSUMER   ——

**SHARE OF
MARKET VOLUME**   ——

LIFETIME   ——

LEVEL OF EXPOSURE   ——

**THIS BRAND IS IDEAL
FOR YOU IF...**   ——

EXAMPLE BRANDS   ——

Author Gaby Arriaga ©

98

WE'VE REACHED THE END OF THIS BOOK.

Our surfing lesson is now over. By this time you are much clearer on what it means to get out into the ocean - that it is not just a matter of willingness, but a matter of knowing how to be there, that the water and its waves behave differently in each stage, and that each stage requires different skills from the person who jumps in. Sometimes you will need to know how to dive, sometimes how to surf, and sometimes it is best just to watch the waves from the shore while you dip your feet in the water.

From the point of view of a company, it is entirely possible to have more than one position and own, for example, a BATHER® brand and a SCUBA DIVER® brand, i.e. a brand that is not very innovative with high sales volumes and another one that is more innovative but sells only to a select few.

Becoming one brand or another is not just destiny, but a responsible choice to be that brand. Not because you were unprepared for the near future, not because you did not anticipate the trends, and not because you let the current take you away. This is paramount.

If you are there because of the circumstances, then where do you want to end up? You may want to stay where you are, and that's okay if it's a conscious decision. However, be sure to communicate that decision to all areas of your company, so that everyone knows what the brand's role is in relation to the trends.

So, whether you're a SCUBA DIVER®, a SURFER®, a FOAM® or a BATHER® brand, what you must never forget is to always stay on top of trends and the near future. Remember the advice parents give to their children the first time they go to the beach: never turn your back on the ocean. Don't let the wave roll over your business while you're distracted by what's happening under your nose, in the present. Look up and see into the near future, which, even if you don't want it to, will arrive. Always live in Near Future Thinking® mode.

CONCLUSIONS

- What reflections or questions have I had while reading this book?
- What are the trends affecting my business, and what stages are they in?
- Where are they and what will my early adopters think?
- Do I have a FOAM® brand? Do I have what it takes to be a SURFER®?
- I know I have a PIÑA COLADA® brand. This can't happen to me again.
- I wanted to be a SURFER® brand, but I think too many things need to change in my company to make it happen.
- I think we are ready to be a SCUBA DIVER® brand.
- Now I know I'm a BATHER® brand and I want to stay there, but in a mindful way.
- We were a SURFER® brand. Now we need to get back to being a SURFER® brand.

If I have succeeded in awakening these kinds of thoughts, I have succeeded in getting you to apply Near Future Thinking® to find the next step for your business.

Near Future Thinking® is a new discipline that considers the near future for decision making. It's a tool to be able to anticipate a future that, like a wave in the ocean, is imminent; it is to be able to decipher how that future will arrive and how to be prepared for it as a company.

The analogy of the ocean always seemed very practical, didactic and even playful to us. Nevertheless, the near future discipline requires that the study of trends be taken more seriously in business. I would like you, as a business decision maker, to discover the profound and meticulous nature of studying the near future and to adopt it as a way of working within your organization. To stop believing that your company is up to date just because you bought a trend report that someone else wrote. And that you make room for a new area specialized in Near Future Thinking® that will work with your Innovation, Research and Development, and Marketing departments continuously. Because becoming one kind of brand or remaining there is a perpetual process. Just as your entire company knows its brand's strategy, it should know its brand's future, and equip that brand with everything it needs to tackle that future, making it the best SCUBA DIVER®, the best SURFER®, the best FOAM® or the best BATHER® brand, but, I insist, NEVER a PIÑA COLADA®.

COMPANY PROFILES OF MEXICAN BRANDS MENTIONED IN THIS BOOK

I. EL 3ER ESPACIO

EL 3ER ESPACIO is a coworking space created by a large community of entrepreneurs. They believe they speak to a new generation that is no longer satisfied with a 9-to-5 job and that sees entrepreneurship as a lifestyle, not just a way to make money. That projects are better when done in collaboration with other people who are passionate and obsessed with a sense of freedom.

EL 3ER ESPACIO is a place for challenging expectations and stereotypes, where workers can make the most of their skills, connections, relationships, knowledge and entrepreneurial spirit.

el3erespacio.mx

—

II. ECOBICI

ECOBICI is Mexico City's public bicycle system that has integrated the bicycle as an essential element of mobility; this mode of transportation was created for the inhabitants of the capital city, its surroundings and tourists.

It allows registered users to take out a bicycle from any station and return it to the station closest to their destination in unlimited 45-minute trips. Those who want to access the ECOBICI system can pay a subscription for one year, one week, three days or one day.

ECOBICI began operations in February 2010 with 84 bike stations and 1,200 bicycles. In eight years, demand has driven the growth of the system, which now operates 480 bike stations and more than 6,800 bicycles, of which 28 stations and 340 bicycles are now part of the new pedal-assist electric bicycle network.

ECOBICI currently has more than 170,000 registered users and the service is available in 55 neighborhoods, in an area of 38 square kilometers.

ecobici.cdmx.gob.mx

III. ECONDUCE

Econduce is an alternative shared mobility system of electric motorcycles that offers users the opportunity to use these motorcycles in strategic points across Mexico City and to park them in their designated locations. The service requires the user to download the company's app in order to locate the nearest motorcycle and charges a monthly subscription fee plus a per-minute rate. It also has a plan for delivery drivers and all drivers are insured against accidents.

econduce.mx

—

IV. LA LONJA MX

La Lonja MX is a traveling design market that promotes contemporary Mexican culture in five yearly editions that offer a direct buying experience between designer and consumer.

The sales categories are objects, furniture, fashion, jewelry, accessories and beauty. Each edition also showcases a rich gastronomic experience that invites the public to enjoy and engage with Mexico's creative culture.

Thanks to its strategy, La Lonja MX has managed to professionalize an entire industry. Over 10 years, La Lonja MX has been a pioneer in creating emblematic spaces in CDMX and a spearhead in the pop-up concept. Its events are a model for Contemporary Mexico, revealing trends, creative processes, ideologies, movements and proposals that would be difficult to come across otherwise.

www.lalonja.mx

V. SÍCLO

A form of high-intensity, stationary indoor cycling. It draws inspiration from spinning, a sport that consists of pedaling at different speeds to the rhythm of loud music. At Síclo, however, cycling is done to a soundtrack of Latin music. All in a semi-dark room without ventilation, which increases sweating.

In addition, Síclo offers a variety of on-site exercise classes, online classes, and now exercise bikes equipped with programs that give you a similar experience to the one you would have in a studio.

siclo.com

—

VI. FUCKUP NIGHTS

Fuckup Nights is a global movement of events where the stories of failure are told by entrepreneurs and business leaders. These events and talks aim to disrupt paradigms about success in business and demonstrate that, through failure, there is always an opportunity for learning and inspiration.

These events are currently held in 185 cities across 64 countries.

fuckupnights.com

BIBLIOGRAPHY
AND
REFERENCES

1. Voros, Joseph, "The Futures Cone, use and history", 2017. <https://thevoroscope.com/2017/02/24/the-futures-cone-use-and-history/>.
2. Voros, Joseph, Swinburne University of Technology, "A Primer on Futures Studies, Foresight and the Use of Scenarios", 2001. <https://thevoroscope.com/publications/foresight-primer/>
3. Rogers, Everett M., Diffusion of Innovations, 5.ª ed., 2003.
4. Schwartz, Shalom H., Are there universal aspects in the content and structure of values?, Journal of Social Issues (The Hebrew University of Jerusalem), vol. 50, no. 4, 1994, pp. 19-45. <https://es.scribd.com/document/209139457/Schwartz-1994-Are-There-Universal-Aspects-in-the-Content-of-Human-Values#scribd>.
5. "Trends after Influenza A (H1N1)-Mexico", Leonardo1452. <https://www.youtube.com/watch?v=3Am4dwTmeEU>.
6. "Erika Boom y el 'fitness' en embarazos saludables". <https://www.pressreader.com/colombia/gente-caribe/20141004/281582353863263>.
7. "My lifestyle". <https://www.fitmama-apparel.com/pages/my-lifestyle>.
8. <https://www.youtube.com/watch?v=6yPfxcqEXhE>. Approximate minute: 46:00 to 46:13.
9. "PandoMonthly: Fireside Chat With Airbnb CEO Brian Chesky". <https://www.youtube.com/watch?v=6yPfxcqEXhE>. Approximate minute: 46:15 to 46:19.
10. "Tendencia Compartir", Leonardo1452. <https://www.youtube.com/watch?v=e5lZpeKjMlk&t=216s>.
11. "Trendoscopio Co-working: El 3er Espacio", Leonardo1452. <https://www.youtube.com/watch?v=2mCB3YbNtF0>.
12. Moore, Geoffrey, Crossing the Chasm. Marketing and Selling High-Tech Products to Mainstream Customers.
13. Gladwell, Malcolm, The Tipping Point.
14. La Lonja MX: <http://www.lalonja.mx/>.
15. Botsman, Rachel. Lo que es mío es tuyo: el surgimiento del consumo colaborativo.
16. "Rachel Botsman: The case for collaborative consumption". <https://www.youtube.com/watch?v=AQa3kUJPEko>.
17. "Sharing. Today's Smart Choice: Don't Own. Share", Time, <http://content.time.com/time/specials/packages/article/0,28804,2059521_2059717,00.html>.
18. "The Many Faces of Influence", Traackr <http://www.traackr.com/faces-of-influence>.
19. "How the Lance Armstrong Foundation Became Livestrong". <https://www.fastcompany.com/1698037/how-lance-armstrong-foundation-became-livestrong>.
20. https://www.makinglovemarks.es/blog/arquetipos-de-personalidad-de-marca/
21. "Google Reveals Its 9 Principles of Innovation". <https://www.fastcompany.com/3021956/googles-nine-principles-of-innovation>.
22. "Browser Market Share Worldwide". <http://gs.statcounter.com/browser-market-share>.
23. "Tips para ser una marca SURFER®". <https://youtu.be/Q6BORN2q5WM>.
24. Arriaga, Gaby, "'Selfies, moda pasajera para las marcas". <http://expansion.mx/opinion/2014/03/27/las-039selfies039-estan-pasadas-de-moda>.
25. "Organizar carreras o maratones se volvió negocio en 10 años". <http://www.milenio.com/negocios/Organizar-carreras-maratones-volvio-negocio_0_418158188.html>.
26. <https://toyota-ai.ventures>.
27. <https://www.recode.net/2016/5/24/11762436/toyota-uber-investment>.
28. <https://media.ford.com/content/fordmedia/fna/us/en/news/2016/03/11/ford-smart-mobility-llc-established--jim-hackett-named-chairman.html>.
29.- Raymond, Martin, The Trend Forecaster's Handbook.
30.- Higham, William, The Next Big Thing.

Made in the USA
Monee, IL
19 September 2023